New Orleans or Sunk!

Also by
Dean E. Felsing

Cobwebs
published 2002

New Orleans or Sunk!

DEAN E. FELSING

abbott press®
A DIVISION OF WRITER'S DIGEST

NEW ORLEANS OR SUNK!

Abbott Press books may be ordered through booksellers or by contacting:

Abbott Press
1663 Liberty Drive
Bloomington, IN 47403
www.abbottpress.com
Phone: 1-866-697-5310

ISBN: 978-1-4582-0091-4 (e)
ISBN: 978-1-4582-0092-1 (sc)

Library of Congress Control Number: 2011919812

Printed in the United States of America

Abbott Press rev. date: 11/14/2011

For Emil

Emil went to heaven several years ago. What a wonderful time he must be having with his interim resurrection body and sound mind. He will never be neglected or have to eat garbage again. How I envy him. Say God, if it can be arranged, I'd like Emil to show me the ropes upon my arrival. I wouldn't even mind picking cotton for him on his estate. Sir, I am ready to join him. Amen.

ACKNOWLEDGMENTS

Thank you to the following for permission to reprint:

Sports Illustrated Magazine

Billy Graham Evangelistic Association

Minneapolis Star Tribune

Center for Global Environmental Education
Hamline University
Rivers of Life
St. Paul, Minnesota
Peggy Knapp and Tracy Fallon

Colin Petit
Cover Design
Also Cover Designer for Cobwebs

For correcting my typos etc.:
Janet Felsing
Bruce Dickinson
Frank Lorentz
Emily Westphal

For Photo Work:
Nathan Felsing
Colin Petit
The Fallon Family Archives

For Research:
Gail Anne Felsing

PREFACE

For "Rear Admiral" John J, Fallon: Expedition Leader and Dear Friend.

Fifty years ago (1961) I had an adventure that was truly extraordinary. Believe it or not I sailed down the Mississippi River from Minneapolis, Minnesota to New Orleans, Louisiana, through ten states and many cities and towns. On of all things, a homemade "raft." At the time I was only fourteen years old and I had had a few scrapes with "John Law." In other words I was what some people called a delinquent. I wasn't a gangster or a bank robber, but I had a tough time at home and that led to troubles in school. I lived in South Minneapolis at the time and was sent by the Juvenile Court system to an experimental program run by Hennepin, County. It was called "The Weekend Program." After school on Fridays a bus would pick up other boys and me at our schools and bring us to a farm near St. Francis, Minnesota until Sunday. There we had several activities and chores like, dish washing, barn cleaning, feeding cows, horse riding and care of the animals and my least favorite activity, group discussions.

The man responsible for getting me to this program was Jo Spano. I still remember the first time I met him. He was fresh out of probation officer school and he had "green" written all over him. I was only eleven or twelve years old and he came to my house in south Minneapolis. I remember he almost had to duck his head to enter our front door. He was the first man I met in my life that didn't seem to have a mean bone in him. We have been true friends now for over fifty years. We have been to jail, court, weddings, funerals, lunches, and even shopping. I love this man and his family to this day and we still chat on the phone. One of the highest honors I have had in my life was to give a speech at Jo's retirement party at the Hennepin County Government Center in front of all the County Commissioners and Judges. Best of all his wife and brother Wy were there. He still advises not only Hennepin County but many counties throughout the state. His picture should be in every dictionary under integrity. Jo Spano and Jack Fallon did more to shape my life above and beyond the call of duty. Jack and Jo were good friends. Jack passed away a few years back and we both miss him very much. Thank you Jo.

These discussions were to help us learn how to cope and deal with problems at home and in school. Some of us learned a few things but most of us just ignored any advice that was offered. Most of the boys were borderline bad. By that I mean they did not need to be locked up in jail, but they did need a guiding hand. The trip that I will be sharing with you was a result of the weekend program and these discussion meetings. It was one of the greatest things that ever happened to me. I learned to work as part of a team, and to work with others even if I did not like them or if I thought that they were perhaps "dumber" than I was. I learned the importance of taking orders without question at times. Following orders can both keep you out of trouble and or save your life; it has mine; in simple every day life in such things as driving an automobile. By following the rules of the road not only will you be much safer, but also so will others.

This trip opened my eyes to many things that I never dreamed possible. The power of the river, the kindness of strangers, the way of life in the South and it showed me that I could do almost anything that I set my mind to and most importantly, how to survive living with about 18 other folks on a very confined space for several weeks.

I believe that each and every boy that was on that trip with me learned something. Whether or not they used the information to better their lives is another matter. Some did wise up if you will. Some sadly did not and wound up in very serious trouble with the authorities. One boy was involved in a famous local kidnapping and when he decided to turn states evidence he was found dead the next day in his jail cell. Another boy was a great lock picker and we got into many places using his talents. I would like you to know that he grew up to be a successful locksmith. Some of the guys were never heard from again. No matter how they wound up each and every one of us must acknowledge a deep debt of gratitude to the weekend program and to its leader Jack Fallon for the respite that the trip gave us from our troubles and woes back home. Thanks Jack.

I still talk with a few of the guys, and we sit back and laugh at our old troubles and adventures and of how things have changed over the years. It would probably not be a good idea to have a reunion of the crew members because some of them still hold a grudge and have stated that they would like to punch some of the others for some such nonsense that happened on the trip. This cannot be a healthy attitude. As far as

I am concerned I only try to remember the good things that happened and not who did what to whom.

When I graduated from high school I wanted to join the Army Corps of Engineers and become a Lockmaster on the Mississippi River. Because I was such a "goof off" in school I could not get in the corps so instead I joined the U S Navy. When I was honorably discharged from the Navy I tried my hand at running a group home for boys who were in the same situation that I was in as a kid. That was one of the toughest things I have ever tried, and I gave it up after about 3 years.

I have had many exciting times running my own businesses over the years. Some examples are being a landlord, a hotel and restaurant I bought in northern Minnesota, a retail store on Lake Street in Minneapolis, and a tour company that specializes in camping trips and tours for developmentally disabled adults. I founded and incorporated Carealot Services (a not for profit organization) in 1976. It was the first of its kind in the United States and was the most rewarding venture I have ever had. Many of the skills that I learned on the raft trip taught me not to panic and for over 30 years was able to share my knowledge of camping and boating with my clients. I loved every minute of it.

Each time I cross the river in my car I remember this great adventure that had such an impact on my life. It is my wish that you will learn some of the lessons that I learned that summer and that you will never give up when things seem impossible for you. I am sure you will have questions as we go along, and hope I can answer as many as you may have. Thank you.

CHAPTER 1

For the Staff and Crew of the Unsinkable

It was the beginning of the school year 1960, I had just turned 14. Ninth grade, and there we sat in a small room, about 15 of us kids and two or three staff members, it was announced to us that we needed to come up with a plan for next summer's vacation. We could do anything within reason and or legal. We were told that if we did not come up with a plan we would spend the summer at the Hennepin County Home School (kid jail) in Glen Lake, Minnesota. For some odd reason this idea appealed to a few of the boys. Well, I remember the first idea, or suggestion, was to ride our horses to the Black Hills in South Dakota. I didn't like the idea; I did not care for horses all that much and I know that my horse, Cindy, did not care all that much for me. I said something to the effect of taking a raft down the Mississippi River. The idea was pushed aside and all the fellas, except me, were excited about the trip to South Dakota.

The very next weekend the man, Max, in charge of the horses spoke to the group. He told us that it was indeed possible for us to accomplish such a trip; the horses were in fine shape and about all we needed to do was prepare. By the time Max got through with the list of things we would have to do to get ready, I knew that I would rather stay at the Home School.

Some of the others felt the same way; it sounded like too much work. Then one of the boys, Eddie, said, "Why not look into the possibilities of the "raft trip". The seed was planted, it would be easy, just toss a few logs together and off we go. At this point I think some of the staff would have been happy to spend the summer at the Home School. I only learned this fact in the year 2000, the head of the weekend program, Jack Fallon, stood in the lodge kitchen with his staff that evening while we were in bed and said that he thought that us boys could pull a raft trip off. I wish I could have been there for that brief moment, I guess it was quite a sight to see the faces of what was to become an incredible crew on an incredible expedition.

The very next weekend we were told to come up with ideas and plans for a "raft". We were all assigned a hand full of town's along the river and we had to write a letter to every city. The letters stated about when we would be through and asked for information on that town, i.e., things like what to see and where to get supplies, gas, and food, etc.

We were enrolled in a water safety class given by the Coast Guard in Minneapolis. Wow, locks and dams. Yup, 26 of them between Minneapolis and St. Louis. After St. Louis there are no more locks and the current is much stronger. The one thing I will never forget from that class was that life jackets are not to save you from drowning, but to make it easier for someone to find your body. We also learned about whirlpools, currents, wing dams, buoys the channel, and much more. We were each given certificates after the classes.

Now for the "raft" itself. None of us had any idea how to build a raft or anything else for that matter. It was decided that we could put a bunch of 55gal oil drums together (somehow) and that would be that. Well, it was not as easy as that. Several ideas were looked at and we found a company that made brackets for just such a raft. These brackets were for people who wanted to put together 4 or 6 drums for a diving dock at the summer cabin. It was the best we could find. The company that made the brackets almost fainted when we told them we were going to put forty oil drums together they immediately told us there was no guarantee on the parts at all. We did get them to donate 80 brackets and wish us luck.

Jack had a few ideas on how to season or toughen us up for the trip. One such fantastic idea was to take us all out in a blizzard and have us make our own dinner. Well, my buddy Jerry and I said, to ourselves of course, "Hell no, we won't go". When the group headed out the front door for the mile or so trek through the woods, Jerry and I headed out the back. We figured it would take a while to notice two missing idiots in a blizzard. We hiked the mile or so to the milk room adjacent to the barn. It was nice and warm in there and we would sit out the outdoor cooking adventure. Jerry sat down and took off his boots and put his feet up toward the stove. I was too scared to be that relaxed. Sure enough, through the flying snow I saw what looked like the Abominable Snowman. It was Jack and the fur around his hood was full of snow and his beard and glasses were frozen. I could tell he was pissed. He walked right past me and grabbed Jerry and thrashed the daylights out of him. I knew I was next. Then Jack asked Jerry why he got "it" and I didn't. Jerry said that it was because he had been at the farm longer than I had. Jack said, "Yes, that's right and next time Dean will get it". I could put it in writing that it would never happen.

As soon as the snow was gone the oil drums arrived at the farm, all forty of them. We laid them out into four rows of ten each with a three foot nose cone to be bolted to the front of each pontoon. The length of the raft would be 33 feet and the width 16 feet. Our fearless leader, Jack, found a house in Minneapolis that had been condemned. He managed to get permission for us kids to rip the insides apart with crowbars and hammers and salvage all the wood that we could carry. This wood became the deck and superstructure. We built the deck in two parts each 8 feet wide. We had a heck of a time getting the drums to stay in place with the brackets, but we managed. The two halves were hauled on a flat bed to the Mississippi River just above the U of M Showboat and just across the river from Fairview Hospital. We then "U" bolted them together and nailed the deck at a diagonal using our salvaged wood. It was starting to look like a real seaworthy vessel. We dubbed it the "Unsinkable". There was a railing out of the 2x4s put all around and a "cabin" of approximately 12' x 12' near the front. It was given a canvas roof and sides that could be rolled up when weather was nice. Around the railing we put chicken wire, which proved to be too weak, it was always being replaced or let go all together. There was a transom put out back and two 40 horse Scott outboard motors were donated. The cables used to steer with were above the deck and the steering wheel was behind the cabin, so the driver could not see where he was going. (One of our smarter moves.) Had OSHA been around we would have been shut down in a flash. At least every one of us tripped on the steering cable a dozen times before we hammered some boards on the deck to stop that hazard. At least then we only tripped on the 2x4s and the driver could still manage to keep us in the channel. By the way, remember the driver could not see where he was going! It took 7+ crew members at any one time to operate the raft. One staff member, to keep the two lookouts (stationed up front) on the ball, and one person to steer and one to navigate, that is read the charts or maps of the river. Believe it or not it is possible to get lost on a river. More about that later. There was also a gas team on call to refuel the main tanks and measure and mix the oil into the gas.

Each of us built a foot locker from our foraged wood, we made drinking cups from soup cans with an attached coat hanger for a handle. Each of us had our own mess kit and we were responsible for it. That meant if we lost it we went without or we had to buy another, now remember we were poor kids and didn't have much if any money. We did not have tents like you see today. We had mosquito netting and a piece of plastic tarp 10'x10' to put over the netting in case of rain. No cook stove either, just a large frying pan and a few pots. We cooked over an open fire or wrapped our food in tin foil and tossed it in the fire until it was done. We loaded up 24 – 5 gallon gas cans, gear, and little knowledge of the adventures that awaited down stream. The Unsinkable was ready for action.

A few days after school let out we met on the banks of the Mississippi and said, "Farewell" to our families.

The Unsinkable

L-R Merle, Dennis, Ron
Author is the short one

Eddie

Froggie & Buddy

CHAPTER 2

For Dennis, Merle, and Ron

Lots of people, even the local news media, down by the riverside to see us off. We were given a flag of the state of Minnesota to give to the governor of Louisiana. We had our gear stowed and our charts out. The staff had agreed not to shave until after the trip and they hadn't done so for some time. So when one of the boys spotted Dennis, clean shaven, the word spread quickly. A few of us went down one side of the deck and a few others took the other side. We then grabbed Dennis and tossed him overboard, right into the river. What a shock, he screamed and hollered, as others were pulling him out of the drink and back on board we spotted his twin brother the, "real" Dennis. He had not shaved. We were off to a grand start, we had our first assault.

Needless to say this didn't make many points with the "real" Dennis. Now, pay attention. This was my first lesson and I seem to learn the hard way. Yes, the School of Hard Knocks. What do you think my lesson was? From then on I always try to look very closely at what is going on and try not to jump to any conclusions. Even if Dennis had shaved that day it was not right for any of us to toss him in the river. Dennis became a counselor at my old high school in Minneapolis, Roosevelt. He is now retired. I must add here that after 50+ years we are still good friends.

Things calmed down and we posed for some photos. Someone made a big sign that said "New Orleans or Sunk!". And we had two signs with "UNSINKABLE" on them. We attached one to the starboard and one to the port after we got under way. Jack, our leader said that if it did sink we would turn it into a submarine and rename it the "UNBELIEVABLE". I don't think many laughed about that, we worked so hard and the thought of it sinking was unimaginable. Never the less, it did look as if it may go under at any time. My son Nathan is a USMC SGT and I would not let him go out on that thing now that I look back.

We had four staff members. One leader/point man, Jack, and three first mates: Merle, Dennis, and Ron. A crew of fifteen boys ages 12 - 15. The plan was for us to get to New Orleans, 1742 miles down the river from Minneapolis. We would then tour the city for a few days and then a replacement crew would meet us and trade places. The replacement crew was only 8 boys and 12 went home via bus. I was one of three to volunteer to stay on and show the new guys the ropes. Plus we needed to lighten the load for the trip upstream.

The Unsinkable was shoved into the current and we were off on the first leg of our journey, the 680 miles to St. Louis, Missouri. It was four miles to the first lock and dam (The Ford Lock & Dam) and Jack took the helm for the first time. We had an air horn to signal the Lockmaster that we wanted to enter the lock. At each dam in the river there is also a lock, this is a very large area that barges and other boats must use to pass around the dam. Any one in a boat or even a canoe may use the locks for free. They are operated by the Army Corps of Engineers. The Drop is anywhere from 4 feet to 27 feet. The drop at the Ford lock was 19 feet.

The huge gates were opened and we entered a lock for the first time. The Lockmaster tossed us two lines (rope) so we would not drift around inside the lock. The gates were slowly closed and the water was let out of the lock through holes in the bottom of it. We went down 19 feet, it was exciting. If you wish you may visit this lock any time in the summer and take a tour. There are also two more locks that were built after our trip, these are the Upper and Lower St. Anthony Falls locks, and you may also visit them.

The Lockmaster sounds a loud horn when it is safe for you to leave the lock. As we left the lock we had our first rhubarb over who was going to steer or pilot the raft. Yes, you can imagine, we all wanted to steer our creation. There were some very loud arguments over who would be next to steer. A list or roster was made and each of us would have a two-hour shift of steering and lookout duty.

Lookout duty was never boring. You had binoculars and a river chart and you had to keep us in the channel. That is between the red, or nun buoys and the black, or can buoys. Even a few feet out of this channel could be very dangerous. You could hit many things that are just under water, tree stumps, or wing dams, a wing dam is an under water dam that directs the water in the river into the channel. You also had to watch for other boats, barges, and floating junk in the water, mostly logs. If we hit or ran over something we usually broke something, most often the steering cable or a sheer pin.

The first thing to break was the shear pin in one of the motors. When this happened we had to switch engines, we usually ran on one engine at a time, then we would head for a safe place to drop anchor or just float along. At first a staff member would jump into the water. Later we all got to be good at this repair. The motor was tilted up and a string was tied to the propeller so that it would not drop to the bottom of the river. Then the prop was removed with a wrench and the broken shear pin was removed and replaced with a new one. This pin was designed to break, because if it didn't, much harm would come to the engine. It only took a few minutes to complete this procedure. But, if there was barge traffic in the area it could get scary from the waves they make as they pass you.

Many, many times during the trip you would hear the cry of "Shear pin" and the shear pin crew would go into action. Well into our journey we didn't even yell, "Shear pin" any more because we all could recognize by the sudden change in the pitch or roar of the engine what had happened and we responded automatically.

The other thing to break was the steering cable. If this happened and we were under way someone had to jump out and hang over the transom and lower the handle on the motor and steer by hand. The lookouts had to be extra vigilant during this time and instructions were shouted to the rear of the raft to the person steering. If the cable or the shear pin broke because the lookouts were goofing off there were severe consequences. They were given the silent treatment, punched by other boys (this was not approved by the staff), or not permitted to eat the next meal. If we were heading to a town to tour they may have been kept on the raft for punishment. Being kept on, or confined to, the raft was not always too bad because as soon as the others were gone you could always sneak ashore and explore on your own. It didn't take long for the staff to figure that out and soon there was a "baby sitter" on board while you were confined to quarters.

As much fun as steering was, it got old. We had to cover at least 100 miles per day and at 10 M.P.H. we had to put in 10 hours per day on the water. This did not take into account for what we called lock time. Lock time could run from 20 minutes to several hours. Barges had priority use of the locks and if a tow with several barges was ahead of us we had to wait. I believe our longest wait was one half of a day. What do you think I learned from this? We used to use this down time to make repairs, and believe me they were always needed, prepare meals, fish, read, write letters home, or plan our next activity.

CHAPTER 3

For Harvey Schroeder

I f you weren't steering, the best place to be was up front. This practice came to a quick halt. If we hit a wave that was over 6 inches we would start to "plough" water, that is, we would actually start to dive under water. The breakers that had been bolted onto the front of the oil drums would fill with water making the front too heavy and we would have to run to the back of the raft to bring it back to level. This was scary the first few times that it happened, and anything that was on the deck got wet. It took a while, but after a few good soakings we learned how to keep the ol' raft trim.

The reason we did not sink was that as soon as we started to plough water the motors were lifted out of the water and they could no longer push us any further into the drink, river that is. Only the lookouts were permitted to be up front and we had a message runner. The message runner could be up front only if he was on business. That business included relaying messages as to where we were and delivering food to the lookouts. Waves on the river could reach 7 feet or more. We had to learn how to ride them, that is to pass over them without getting wet or breaking anything.

We were on a part of the river called Pigs Eye; this is just below St. Paul, when we spotted a tow with several barges going up stream. What fun it would be to ride the waves that were created by its wake. Just about a mile or so behind such barges a large wave called a "king wave" follows. The bigger the barges, the bigger the king wave. This was a big one. Perhaps 12 or more barges tied or lashed together. We spotted the king wave and decided to ride it. The raft, much to our surprise did not even raise one inch, instead the king wave went over us like we weren't even there. The raft wobbled like a flour tortilla. I was sure we were all as good as dead.

It tore off the entire front railing and ruined some other parts. This included the screen on the front of the cabin and broke the steering cable, the first time of many times. We were lucky we didn't end up in the water. We had an instant learning experience and from then on we never went behind any barges. We also gained a healthy respect for the river and its' powers.

You may be interested to know a little more about tows and barges. First, a towboat does not tow anything, it pushes. It pushes barges. It pushes from one up to 24 barges at a time. The barges are tied or lashed together with wire ropes, these ropes are held together with huge clasps much like a very large clasp on a necklace. To unhitch these clasps a deck hand uses a heavy sledge hammer. This is a very dangerous occupation and the men and women are trained and use much skill on the job. They live on the towboats all summer long and they really love the river life.

We made many friends with these people, some of them helped to save our lives. It was awesome to watch these barges pass our campsites at night with their engines roaring and the powerful spot lights. Sometimes we could get the Captain to shine the spotlight on us as we ran up and down the sand bars and wave at the crew on board. What fun.

Well, now we had our first repairs to make. We also had to dry out. How about that, we weren't even underway for more than an hour or so and we were wet, broken, and scared. I think some of us wished we were at the home school. First thing was to get the steering cable back in order. While some of us worked on that, others worked on the broken railing and replacing the screen in the cabin. The rest of us hung up our clothes and sleeping bags to dry out. Boy did we look funny floating down the river on a broken raft with all that laundry hanging on the rails and from ropes that we tied from the roof to the railings. We passed our first test and learned our first lessons as sailors. But, we weren't able-bodied seamen yet.

CHAPTER 4

For Eddie, Molly, Mary E., and Dennis Fallon

Not only did we look funny, we looked pathetic. We looked like a floating Laundromat that had an explosion in it. Here we were on our brand new raft and we were a mess. The repairs were made to the steering cable and we would have to wait to get parts for the railing and the screens and chicken wire. The clothes and sleeping bags would dry sooner or later in their own time.

Remember the channel I mentioned earlier? The channel is like a road in the water and it is marked by buoys and lights. The channel is maintained at nine feet deep by the Corps of Engineers. It is several hundred feet wide. All you had to do was stay between the buoys and you would be safe. This is called navigating. The navigator would look at the charts and tell the driver which way to go, and the lookouts would make sure we stayed between the buoys and didn't hit anything. Most of the time, that is.

In the daytime you could see the buoys very easily. At night there were blinking lights called oscillating lights. In the dark it was difficult to see the buoys so you would head for the nearest blinking light until another one came into view, then you would head for the new light. This would keep you in the channel. On each light there was a sign with the miles on it, much like the number you see on the freeway when you travel by car. The number was the number of miles that you were from the mouth of the Ohio River. After the Ohio River the mile number was your distance from the mouth of the Mississippi River or the Gulf of Mexico.

Now, with all this help you would think we would have little trouble getting to our destination. Well, guess again. Our next lock was lock and damn #2 at Hastings, Minnesota. Just a few miles from where we hit the king wave. The river was just over a mile across and we could see a wide-open river ahead, so we decided to take our first short cut. After all, if you could see where you wanted to be way off to your right and the channel went to the left, why not head directly for the lock? This would perhaps shave off a few miles and precious time. The lookouts aimed us directly at the lock about 5 miles ahead.

Our short cut took us right through an underwater stump field. This was created many years ago when the dam was built and the river backed up over a wooded area. The trees were all gone now and all that was left was the stumps. We were just a few hundred feet into this submerged forest and all of a sudden the first cry of "shear pin". Then we broke our steering cable again. It was like being in a minefield except that the stumps did not blow up. It took us several hours and more shear pins to work our way back into the channel. The eeriest thing was to hear the stumps constantly pounding on our oil drum pontoons, there was just no avoiding them.

Ah yes, another lesson on the river. Can you guess what this one was? We couldn't really blame any one but ourselves for this blunder. Most of the time we tried to pin the blame for things that went wrong on someone else even if it was your fault you would do your best to blame the next guy. Ain't human nature grand? Remember, most of us had been together for over a year by now and we pretty well knew who was responsible for what. For the most part I got along with the majority of the other boys. In fact some of us lived near enough to each other that we would play together after school and on weekends when not on the farm. We did things like swat pigeons under the Broadway Avenue Bridge over the Mississippi in north Minneapolis. If we caught a pigeon we would put it in a paper bag and get on a city bus and let it go. Now you know one of the reasons that I got into trouble. It wasn't very nice with all the feathers and poop flying around inside the bus, but it sure was a heck of a lot of fun.

Lock and dam #2. Jack, our leader, went ashore and got his car. He mostly followed us in the car so he could go ahead and make arrangements for publicity, food, repairs, things to see and other things we may need. I do think he needed to get away for a while, especially now that we got him soaked and damaged most of the front end of the Unsinkable and all the hubbub over the steering and getting lost in the stump field. Gee whiz, we had only been on our voyage for less than a few hours, us boys hadn't even begun to get even for things we held against society, thus far every thing was gratis.

Jack was an excellent scrounge. By this I mean he could find anything, even if it wasn't there. Yes, he was a magician. In fact most of the things that our craft was made out of were "found" by this man. He scoured the Twin City area high and low and asked for donations from the most unusual sources. I think some people gave him things, like the oil drums and lumber and nuts and bolts just so he would go away.

By go away I mean because his story about a raft and the river and all was too much for some people. After all, no one in their right mind would take 15 delinquent boys down the Mississippi River on a good day, on a battleship, let alone let them build their own vessel and take on Mother Nature. How he got the folks at the outboard motor company to donate two out board motors is still a mystery to me. These people ended up giving us a total of five engines. More about this down the river. He also got a major oil company to donate all of our gas and oil. This remarkable fellow became one of my best friends and for many years after the raft trip we sat at his house many times and would tell and retell the stories of our river adventures.

I learned many things from the river and Jack, and hope that some day you may have as good a friend as I found in this man and his family. I must add at this point that in early 1964 I was in jail and had no where to go. I had been kicked out of high school and I refused to go home. My future was not very bright and I was sitting in front of yet another juvenile judge. Jack was in the court room. He asked the judge if he could have a moment to call his wife, Lucy, to get her permission to take me in until a foster home could be found for me. Lucy said, "Yes" and I was spared going to jail. Jack managed to get me into Roosevelt High School and into a foster home with Henry and Mildred Stivlund. I did graduate that summer in 1964 and was asked by Hennepin County if I would go on yet another raft trip from Minneapolis to St. Louis and return via the Mississippi River. They offered me the job of cook and would pay me $2.00 per week. I said "Yes" in a heart beat.

I can never say thanks enough to the Fallon or the Stiveland families. I still visit Lucy Fallon and her children and grandchildren, they have all encouraged me to write this story for you.

CHAPTER 5

For Gail, Nathan, and Molly Felsing

We entered lock #2 at Hastings, Minnesota. When the Lockmaster, that's the man in charge of the lock and dam, saw us he wondered what it was that he saw. He asked us a few questions and when he heard us say that we were headed for New Orleans he almost fell into the lock. It didn't look like we could make it out of the lock or even to Hastings just one mile down stream. As we left the lock after the loud whistle, I could see him shaking his head. He told us that he would notify the next Lockmaster at lock #3 that we were on the way.

This became a great way to communicate. All of the Lockmasters looked forward to our arrival, especially after we made the first few locks in one piece. Hastings, Minnesota was our first stop. Before we went ashore we set up a buddy system and were each assigned a buddy. This was to keep us together and if we ever needed help we could rely on our buddy. Usually our buddy was also our tent mate. At least this way we usually got along.

Before we were allowed to roam the town we had to complete our chores. They ranged from carrying gas and food and water to tying up the raft at the dock or marina. Remember, a river is always moving, unlike a lake, so if you don't tie up your craft right it will get away from you. Every water craft must face up stream when tied up at a dock. We didn't have to be told this too many times to get it through our thick skulls.

My buddy Eddie was a skinny red-haired kid and just a little taller than me. He was what you may call a laid back kid. He was so nice that I can't imagine him getting into any trouble. Unless he got a kick out of the pigeon stunt I don't think Eddie was much of a problem to society at all. Eddie and I got along great and usually stood lookout together. Eddie was the boy who spoke up and said, "Why not give the raft trip a try?' To think we are still buddies after 50 years. Thanks Eddie, I love ya.

We did a lot of exploring and when we did go ashore in the towns, the first thing we did was look for pop bottles. Pop bottles were worth only .02 cents back then, but we could usually pick up enough bottles to buy a candy bar or bottle of pop to stick in our footlocker for later in the day or in the middle of the night. What a treat.

Fifteen boys therefore 7 teams of buddies and one left over. If there ever was an odd amount of an item such as food, candy, or pop we played a game we called "Horsengoggle." Any boy who wanted in on the goodie would stand in a circle with the others and one boy would count to three. On the count of three each boy would hold up 1 - 5 fingers. The fingers were totaled up and the Horsengogglee, if you will, would count from one to the number of fingers, starting on his right, the person that he ended up with received the item. As there was no way to cheat in this "game" it was the fairest system we had and there never was any argument over who won. By gollie one thing we got right.

Each buddy team was responsible for their own tent pitching. Putting up your tent, really a mosquito net, was fairly simple. First you would find a nice level spot of ground, usually sand. Then one or both of the buddies had to find two stakes to keep the netting up. After chopping something that resembled a tree you would put the netting over the two poles and put sand all around the edges. You also had to hurry and get your belongings into the tent before the mosquitoes did.

Then if you were fortunate, it did not rain and then all you had to do was fight off the sand fleas and chiggers. One thing we learned right off the bat was not to camp on the west banks of the river, because if you did and there were no clouds the next morning, the sun would cook you like a hot dog. So, unless we were really soaked from the day before we would make camp on the east side of the Mississippi.

As I have mentioned each of us had a mess kit, canteen, sleeping bag, and other items such as a pocket knife, a drop line for fishing, some of us had cameras, and a 10 - 12 foot piece of rope. We made this rope ourselves back at the weekend farm. We made it from baler-binder twine used on the farm to bale hay. It was a very simple process.

First we would place an old chair outside and attach a 1x6x16 board across the back of it. The board had three holes drilled through it and another board of 1x2x24, also with three holes, we called this the crank handle. We would place three coat hangars through the holes and bend them so that they had a hook on one end and you could turn the smaller board like a handle. We then took the twine and tied it to an end hook and ran it to the length we wanted. This had to be somewhat longer than the finished length because the rope would "shrink" as it was twisted. We would run the twine back and forth several times until the desired width. Six strands would yield ¼ inch and twelve strands would = ½ inch and so on.

On the far end one boy would stand holding a Y shaped stick. As the twine was spun it would automatically come off the other end, at the Y stick, and the finished product was a nice strong rope. Before the rope was used we would singe it with fire to burn off all of the fine threads that stuck out. We really did become experts at this. After the singeing of our new rope we had a good tug of war with it to remove any and all kinks. It was a tedious task and after what seemed to be several million feet of rope we didn't look forward to making any more.

As I said each of us had our own rope, which I will call line from now on, because once on the water rope is called line. We also had two 50-foot lengths and several spare lines. These long lines were used to tie us to the beach at night. Each corner of the raft had a line for docking and we had two anchor lines. We dragged the rope making machine along and a role of twine just in case.

We made our own anchors, out of all things, old coffee cans. We would fill the bottom of the cans with rocks and we mixed cement and poured it over the rocks to the top of the can. Then while the cement was still wet we would insert a piece of wire that was used for wiring from the house we helped to demolish. It had a loop in it so we could attach our lines. These anchors were great for rowboats, but weren't worth the rocks that were in them for the raft. Remember, we are not even finished with our first day. So stay tuned, you won't believe what happens next.

CHAPTER 6

For Dr. Titus P. Bellville

Lock and dam #3, Red Wing, Minnesota. The Lockmaster was waiting for us. The Lockmaster from Hastings had sent word. The gates were open wide and we passed through in 15 minutes. We were getting the hang of it. Just below Red Wing, the St. Croix River enters the Mississippi. You can actually see the two rivers mix. If you ever visit Prescott, Wisconsin make sure that you go to the riverbank and watch these two great rivers blend together.

From Red Wing to the Minnesota border is the most scenic of any on the entire river. With the high bluffs and egrets, blue herons, and eagles. We also saw many animals like deer, raccoons, porcupines, and snakes. We did not stop in Red Wing as we were running late and the weather was starting to turn bad. We would look for a campsite on Lake Pepin. This lake is really part of the river that runs for 21 miles and is just over 2 miles across, it's big and very little current. For lunch the first day we had packed our own from home, but that was gone and we were hungry, tired, and wet. The storm came upon us so fast we didn't have time to get to shore.

You could not see across the deck. The staff passed out the life jackets and we tied down every thing that was loose. We had our lights on and hoped that we would not get run over by a barge. Then came the cry of "shear pin" and our steering cable broke again. We dropped the anchors. They lasted three minutes. They were too small and light to hold us in place. The raft spun slowly around several times. Suddenly we came to a halt in the middle of the river. We were now out of the channel and hung up on a sandbar. We were lost. It was weird to be in the middle of a river and yet be only ankle deep in water.

It was too far to swim for help so we decided to ride out the storm on the sandbar. We had some bread and peanut butter and we ate that up. Boy was it good. We had our sleeping bags over us to keep us warm and all we could do was to sit and wait. Remember the roof of our cabin was made of canvas, well, it leaked, I don't know what else we expected with the 8,000 nails we used to keep it in place.

Several hours later the wind died down and we decided to get the raft off of the sandbar. All hands except the driver went overboard. The raft was way too heavy for us to move, but with all of us in the water it made just enough difference so we could rock the raft like you would a car stuck in the snow. After about 20 minutes we got her free. Big deal, we were still lost and it was about midnight. We headed for what we thought was shore, but we did not know if we were on the Wisconsin or Minnesota side.

We also during this time had to have crossed the channel at least once. This is not very smart because barges run all the time and in any weather. It is a miracle we didn't get run over. Then someone yelled for us to shut up and turn our engines off. Low and behold through the night we could see a flashlight and could hear a voice calling. We headed for it and it was Jack, our leader. He had been searching for us for hours. What a relief. We pulled into shore at a place we learned the next day was Wacouta Beach, on the Minnesota side of the river. We made camp and slept like rocks. Like rocks that were still going up and down that is. We didn't have our sea legs yet, but that would come.

CHAPTER 7

For Joseph P. Spano Jr.

Rise and shine. Thank goodness the weather had cleared up and the sun was out. Everything we owned was soaked; even the driftwood we gathered wouldn't burn. For breakfast we had cold cereal and apples or bananas, and rolls. Some one made a bucket of orange juice. If things had been dry we would have cooked bacon and eggs or some hot oatmeal. Some days Eddie and myself got up early and caught a bunch of frogs and had frog legs for our breakfast. We really knew how to live. Some of the boys caught fish and ate them.

For lunch we usually had sandwiches on the raft, and if we were in a town we were given fifty to seventy five cents to buy our own food. This was plenty of money back then and you could get a hamburger, fries, and pop and still have enough to buy a candy bar for a later treat. As for the rest of the food, we were given what we called "commodities". This was free food from the government for welfare people and seeing that all of us were poor we qualified for the commodities. Most of this food was good, but to this day, I can't eat pinto beans. Some of this food was peanut butter, canned meat (like Spam only worse), cheese, flour, sugar, pinto beans, and my favorite, powdered milk. YUCK! I am sure it was all left over from some grandiose war.

We wanted to stay and dry out, but we were behind schedule and in need of several repairs. Jack left us again and we agreed to meet in Lake City, Minnesota ½ way through Lake Pepin. There was little to no current and we only made about 4 - 5 M.P.H. and it took us 3 hours to get to Lake City. It was decided that we were too heavy and something had to go. One of the boys suggested the anchors could be tossed, but we decided to keep them. They would come in handy for tying up the raft at night if you wrapped the lines around a tree and attached an anchor to them at least they would not unwind and it saved us tying knots.

It was decided that the footlockers would go. This would lighten our load by about 400 pounds. This was difficult for us because we had each (including the staff) made our own and they were all unique. Jack scrounged some army surplus duffel bags and we stowed our belongings in them. We stopped in the Lake City marina, this is like a parking lot for boats, and the staff gave us some money for lunch and some volunteers helped to repair the Unsinkable. After several hours and having explored all there was in Lake City, it was back to the newly repaired raft.

Wow, new railings, new chicken wire, new screens, and some great handy man from town fixed the steering cable, heavy duty. We were off, and as we slipped into the channel we gave the first of many of three cheers to the folks at the marina. One boy would yell, "Hip, hip" and the rest of us would yell, "Hooray". We repeated this three times, it was our way of saying thank you.

The going was still slow as we still had the footlockers on board, and we were in the middle of the lake. Soon we reached the area where the Chippewa River enters the Mississippi. We were back in the current and in the channel. Now to find a place to camp and cook our first supper on shore. We found a sandbar and tied up the raft. We used the footlockers for the fire to cook on. I am pretty sure a few tears were shed at this meal.

CHAPTER 8

For Emil Koivisto

After a good night rest we ate and broke camp. Did I mention how wet we were? Did I mention the canvas roof and sides? Well, things were drying out now and do you have any idea how much canvas shrinks when it dries? The flaps that covered the sides once reached the deck, but now were at least 6 inches higher or shorter. In case I forget to tell you later; by the end of the trip the canvas did not even reach far enough to cover the screens. In all it shrunk over 2 feet.

We were always stopping for bathroom breaks and this was slowing us down. We decided that a toilet would be nice. With that we chopped a hole in the deck in the right front corner of the cabin and built up the sides with 2x4s and then topped it off with a toilet seat. At this point I believe every fly on the river got wind of this great invention and after ten days you could not get within two feet of the toilet. It may have taken only five days to happen, I really don't remember, but I do remember it had to go. So we flushed the toilet down itself and covered the hole with a piece of plywood.

This came in handy. You see in the marinas it was illegal to fish, for at least two reasons. First, the marina owners did not want their paying customers to get hurt. Second, fishing line can really ruin a prop or your motor. This never stopped us, all we had to do was lift the plywood and we could fish as much as we wanted. Ah yes, nothing like catching your lunch in a toilet.

One of the boys we called Froggy was a dead ringer for the boy who played Froggy on the Little Rascals. I knew him for over a year before I learned his real name, Bob. This kid was funny and a hard worker. He was not afraid of anything and a great crew member. One day an item of his went overboard when a wave caught us by surprise. I think it was his cup and it washed right off the back of the raft. You never saw a kid get so upset. After several items of clothing and miscellaneous stuff washed overboard, we decided that a lookout was needed to watch the rear and stop things from ending up in the drink.

This was a job none of us wanted. If an item was lost due to your negligence you were in a heap of trouble. This included tearing up your tent in the middle of the night or a sever thrashing from the person whose item was lost. This happened a few times, but after a while nothing got off that raft. By the way, this was the only lookout that also had to wear a life jacket at all times, just in case he had to dive after something or lost his balance. After much complaining we built a chicken wire fence across the aft end. I am not real sure, but I have a sneaking hunch that may have saved a life.

Some of the gear we had aboard was donated for experimental purposes. One such item was a mosquito repellent that was invented by two brothers and they gave us two cases of this stuff to try out. It was called Zizz. This stuff sent a signal to every mosquito within an entire five county area. The only way you could kill a mosquito with it was to clobber it with the bottle. Not only did it not work, it stung your eyes worse than mace, now don't ask me how I know that.

A few of the boys smoked cigarettes and some of the boys stole these from one another. One day a fight broke out over a stolen cig and of all things used as a weapon they chose Zizz. I never saw such a fight in my life, I think everyone on board got into the fray. Yes, even the staff got into this one. One of the reasons for this was that even a drop of Zizz would make your face burn and the stuff was flying everywhere and if you got it on you, you had to strike back. Every one had at least two or three bottles of Zizz and it was terrible.

Some of us jumped overboard just to stop the stinging. We all had red faces for quite a while after and we had to pull ashore to wash up and get our sight back. Our staff confiscated all of the Zizz and tossed it overboard. Now we had to use our fists we were told, or learn not to steal from one another. Ya right, I still knew where there was a few bottles of Zizz. Not only that, I have a 20 dollar bill that says I can still lay my hands on a bottle of that crap 50 years later.

CHAPTER 9

For Jimmy, "My Dad" Jimmy

One team of boys were two Mikes. I'll call them Mike A. and Mike B. One was very quiet and I'm sure he did more than lurk with intent to loiter to get into the weekend program. The other Mike was a very bright and witty fellow. He kept morale high. He always had a come back to everything you said. He was great to listen to, an early Don Rickles. However, this took its toll on the staff. There was no way to get this youngster to shut up.

Yes, I really admired him. Just when things got rough, good ol' Mike B. had something hilarious to say. I have included a picture of him flinging some of his food overboard with his fork. This was shocking to me because I was always being yelled at to not waste food, even commodities. Yet here stood this boy taking one fork full at a time and tossing it into the river followed by a comment on its quality, or lack there of.

It was this boy who invented our "washing machine". Of course, our clothes got dirty and needed cleaning. Mike B. started a laundry business. He would charge from .05 cents to .15 cents to do a load of soiled whatever. He simply put some soap in your pockets and or your socks, and crammed your clothes into an onion or potato bag and would drag it over the side for about ½ an hour. What amazes me is that he never lost anything and it worked. What scares me is that, today he may be designing parts for airplanes.

Winona, Minnesota and on our way to La Crosse, Wisconsin. We were held up at lock and dam #7 and the weather was getting rough again. We were ready this time and had all our gear tied down ahead of time. It was a good thing because this storm almost did us in. We stayed in the channel, but we really took a thrashing. The new steering cable held fast and we kept in control of the raft. Right about then the horse trip seemed like the best idea. I heard someone yell out, "Who's idea was this?" Not one person onboard cried or said that they wanted to go home, by gollie, we built this thing and we were going to make it to New Orleans.

We arrived in La Crosse, Wisconsin and Jack came aboard. Then we headed up river a little way to Taylor Island and made camp. That had to be one of the greatest nights that I spent on the trip. Jack and the staff kept us up all night telling us tall tales and jokes. We sang songs and seemed to forget about the weather. At this point the staff may have been trying to soften us up to tell us that we may not make it to our destination. But after watching us work as a team they decided to go on. And that we did.

We were now 150 miles from home. Next morning the weather was great, we had our clothes hung out to dry and we were off. We stopped just above lock and dam #8 at Genoa, Wisconsin and climbed the bluffs and looked up and down the river. Gee, what a view, you can see three states from the top of the bluff, Minnesota, Wisconsin, and Iowa. We were really under way.

Lynxville, Harpers Ferry, Prairie Du Chien, and then Guttenberg, Iowa. We stopped for supplies and looked around town. As people heard of our arrival in some of these towns they would come out and greet us and many took us on tours. We rode in everything from cars, a Boy Scout truck, a school bus, and yes even a paddy wagon. Many people gave us food, or if it was a Sunday and we attended church, many times we would have a picnic with the congregation after the service.

This was due to Jack being the point man and stirring up publicity for us. As usual the people received three cheers. Dubuque, Iowa. What a great city. I had seen pictures of a cable car from there and Eddie and I went off to find it. It was called the Fenelon Place Elevator, dubbed the world's shortest, steepest, scenic railway. All of 296 feet to the top and a great view of the city and the river. It cost .05 cents to ride up and down the bluff. What a great memory.

Bellevue, Savanna, Fulton, Clinton, Illinois. What a stop! The mayor was at the dock to greet us and so was the local newspaper. We were taken on a tour of the MoorMan research company. Acres and acres of land used for seed experiments. All of their research was for farmers and agriculture. They treated us to a feast in the company cafeteria. I don't understand why they were so nice to us, we sure weren't ever going to buy any of their seeds.

It was a great time and got us away from the river for the day. That evening there was a carnival in the streets of downtown Clinton and we were invited to stay. We were given free passes to every ride and free hot dogs and pop. I am sure that none of us had ever been given the red carpet treatment in our lives before that day. It felt good and made us feel important. During the carnival many people stopped us and asked questions about the raft and the river. It sure was great to be liked by so many people we didn't even know.

Then Le Claire, Wisconsin and the quad cities, Moline, Bettendorf, Rock Island, and Davenport, next stop, Muscatine, Iowa. Right out of lock and dam #16 is Muscatine, Iowa. On the docks there was a group of people waiting for us. We were given tours of two button companies. At that time Muscatine was known as the button capitol of the world. Most of the buttons were made out of mother of pearl that had been harvested from the Mississippi River. How fascinating to learn how these items were produced. I still have the samples that were given to each of us.

Burlington, Iowa and then Fort Madison, Iowa. We landed in Fort Madison and there was another crowd waiting. Wow, we were getting famous. We had a tour of the state prison by the warden himself. We got to talk with the inmates and I'll tell you one thing, after that tour, I knew that I never wanted to end up in a cell, ever.

We also toured the Schaffer Pen Company. Each of us got to hold a 100 ounce gold bar that was used in the making of some of the ink pens. They gave each of us a cartridge pen and pencil set. I gave this to my mother after the trip and she still uses it to this day. There is a lot of history connected to this part of the river and we learned of the Mormon crossing 100 years ago from Nauvoo, Illinois. That is where we headed for next.

As we left the marina at Fort Madison there were huge black clouds ahead and we thought if we hit one more storm that it would be the end for certain. Closer and closer and all of a sudden they hit us. They were not rain clouds, but clouds of Mayflies, worse than any storm. We could not see across the deck and they were in our hair and eyes and everything else. We covered ourselves with our mosquito netting and tried to stay in the channel. This lasted for about an hour, but it seemed like forever. For days after the river and the city streets were covered with dead Mayflies and, holy cow, did they stink.

Nauvoo was a nice town and we had a tour and picnic and went for a swim with some of the kids form the area. There was a sunken towboat here also and we dived all over it.

Keokuk, Iowa, lock and dam #19 the largest on the river. We were in awe. It was a 29 foot drop and had the largest locks on the river. We were now entering Missouri. We had our sea legs and were on our way to becoming sailors, or at least able bodied seamen.

CHAPTER 10

For my uncle: Machinist's Mate, William Felsing, U.S.S. Pennsylvania, Pearl Harbor, Survivor. Dec. 7, 1941

Missouri, land of fireworks, Mark Twain, President Harry S. Truman, The Unsinkable Molly Brown, and don't forget, even more fireworks. You could not buy fireworks legally in Minnesota, so we went nuts buying every kind of explosive that you could imagine. Remember we carried up to 140 gallons of gas onboard? Well, we didn't blow up the raft, but we damn near blew each other up.

One boy lit a firecracker and another boy yelled for us to duck. The boy with the lit firecracker did not realize that this warning was for his lit firecracker and he covered his head with his arms and the thing exploded in his ear. So, no more firecrackers on the raft! The only other close call we had with fire was when one boy sneaked a cigarette under his sleeping bag while he sat on top of the gas cans. The punishment was swift. We pulled ashore and formed a line and this guy had to crawl between our legs as we took turns hitting him with sticks that we gleaned from the nearby woods. I wonder if he quit smoking after that?

One other problem we had was with the wiring. We had a battery for the running lights and the outboards recharged it as we went along. This battery was too close to the gas cans and one day an alert boy jumped for the fire extinguisher and emptied it on the battery, it had shorted out and caught fire. He was our hero for quite some time.

We made camp just above Hannibal, Missouri. Then we went into town. It was July 3rd and there was a large crowd there to greet us at the marina. We saw everything. The townspeople and local Jaycees took us to the Mark Twain house, Molly Brown's house and many other sites. We were also taken to the Mark Twain cave a little ways out of town and given a guided tour through it. They gave us a great picnic after our cave tour.

We went back to our camp that night and spent the next day seeing more of Hannibal. That night we watched the fireworks display and were mobbed by the townspeople asking us questions and shaking our hands. One area kid even wanted our autographs. The mayor came down to the marina to wish us well on our continued journey. It was a very hot day and we sang "Jingle Bells" for the mayor and the crowd of well-wishers. They also receive three cheers for their kindness. Once again we hit the newspapers. This was getting to be a habit.

It was time to get underway. St. Louis, Missouri was our next port of call. 125 miles away. A piece of cake. We sailed all day and camped just above Alton, Illinois not far from Lewis and Clark's first winter camp before they set off for the great west. That was 1804, 157 years before we passed through there. The next morning we packed up and went through the chain of Rocks Channel that led to the last lock and dam on the Mississippi River #26.

The first thing you notice is how much the current picks up. Upstream the current was 5-6 M.P.H. and now it was 10-12 M.P.H. You had to learn how to steer all over. And it took a great deal of strength. Our steering shifts were cut down from two hours to one hour. We also changed charts. The upper Mississippi charts were small and easy to hold, the LMVD (Lower Mississippi Valley Division) charts were large and had lots more detail in them. More to see and learn.

Now we could see the skyline of St. Louis. We gave ourselves three cheers. It was like winning a million bucks. The reality did not sink in right away. We noticed a huge riverboat on the banks. It was a side-wheel paddle boat for tourists. It's name was the Admiral. There were other showboats and over all it looked pretty dumpy and seedy. Jack met us at a marina and had made arraignments for us to stay at the YMCA in downtown St. Louis. I remember one evening reporters standing out on the sidewalk interviewing us boys from our second floor rooms.

The Chevrolet Company gave us three brand new station wagons to use while we stayed in St. Louis. We stayed several days and saw the Zoo, the Transportation Museum, a barge manufacturing company, and a towboat manufacturing company, and Checker Board Square, where we were each given red and white checkered shirts. We toured the Chevrolet plant in East St. Louis, Illinois. I remember that they would not let us see the place where Corvettes were made, top-secret stuff I guess.

We were taken to Busch Gardens and given free passes and food. The staff had a well-earned rest and a few free beers. We even got a three-hour ride down the river on the Admiral. There was a live big band aboard and we danced and ate, it was fantastic.

We also had an unexpected look at the river we would soon pass on our raft. We saw many historic places and learned so much history.

We met with the mayor and were in the papers. During this time of touring and rest, the raft was under going repairs and preventative maintenance. Always something.

When we left Minneapolis the raft deck was very flat or level. Now it was noticeably bowed. Not sagging, but bending so that the center of the deck looked like a small hill. A heavy duty railing was added to the rear deck so nothing would wash overboard and as the river was more wicked, we had to be extra careful. Our props had also been chewed up and needed replacing. These props were very expensive. I don't know now much they cost, but I do remember the staff talking to us about taking it easy and being more careful on lookout duty.

Now it was time to go. What a fantastic time, what nice people. As I watched Jack, Dennis, Ron and Merle, I think deep down they were impressed and even a little amazed that such a rag tag crew of misfits had got this far.

CHAPTER 11

For Henry Morton Stanley and Dr. David Livingston, who led Henry to the Lord.

The river has taken on a dramatic change. The bluffs were gone and the towns were fewer. The barges were bigger and the wing dams were visible and the current was fast and strong. We were now into the South and the people and customs and scenery were all new to us. Spanish moss was hanging from the trees and we swung from vines like Tarzan in the woods when we camped. We were referred to as Yanks as much as we were called Huck Finns. Back home we called Coke and root beer, pop, down here they called it soda. We said beer was on tap and they said it was on draught. And of course the ever famous "you all".

As I have mentioned, we had some experimental tasks to perform on board. One of them involved the engines that had been given to us. We were using an oil mixture of 40:1. The usual mix at the time was 10:1. We each learned how to clean and gap spark plugs. We also kept a log of the amount of time that was on each motor. Today most outboard motors use the 40:1 or better mixture and I like to think we had a part in the development of this way to save on fuel. However, this was the beginning of this mixture and I believe that it took its toll on the motors, that and so did the pitch of the props. The props we were using were pitched for speed and we needed a power pitch. In the end, the outboard company learned that two 28 horse power motors pitched for power beat the two 40 horse ones we had been using. In St. Louis the props were changed to a different pitch, for more power, however we kept the same 40 horse engines. That is why they were so expensive. They did not do the trick and soon one of the motors froze. It was beyond repair. The company sent us a new one and had it installed as soon as we hit the next town, I am sorry I do not recall the name of that town. We also learned how to file the damaged props back into usable condition.

The first time in the now new faster current, that we pulled into to make camp we were hauling the raft ashore using the long corner lines and it got away from us. The current was so strong it pulled the lines right our of our hands. Fortunately there were two boys and one staff still on board and they went into action immediately. The staff lowered the motors into the water and the boys pulled in the lines. They had to act fast because if they hit a wing dam on this part of the river the raft would break into pieces. The motors were started and they swung the Unsinkable around and into the current. They had to continue down stream for a while to gain control of the raft and we on shore had a few moments of anxiety as they disappeared from our sight. About five minutes later they returned, a little pale and shaken, but in one piece, they received three cheers. From then on there would be at least two boys on each line and there would be no more swimming in the river.

One really neat phenomenon was the wing dams. Up river, as I said they were underwater, here they were made out of telephone poles and rose twenty to thirty feet above the surface of the river and usually about 50 - 60 of them in a row. If you lit a firecracker the echo from the wing dam sounded like someone dragging a stick along a picket fence. It was fun to listen to and we used up most of our fireworks just to hear this sound.

Cape Girardeau, Missouri. A large city and we got off and goofed around for about ½ day. One of the boys found a wounded pigeon and brought it back to the raft. Our staff told us it would probably die, but we pleaded to keep it and they gave in. Well, the thing lived and we named him Girardeau, in honor of that city. Girardeau not only lived he stayed with us for some time and he was never confined to a cage. I believe he was waiting to mend completely and knowing we meant him no harm he stayed. He would fly around us on the river and gave us something else to think about rather than ourselves.

Cairo, Illinois and the mouth of the Ohio River. Half way. There was an eight-mile stretch of straight channel ahead and Jack ordered the engines to be shut down. We all gathered in the center of our bowed ship and Jack delivered a speech I will never forget. He told us that this was the half way point and that if we didn't make it one more mile the entire trip was a success and that none of us were failures. He told us how proud he was of each and every one of us. He complemented each one of us on our growth and team effort. For some of these boys it was the first time in their lives they had ever been successful at anything. We felt good about ourselves and were ready to continue.

I really feel that Jack didn't think we were going to make it to New Orleans, he knew something that we didn't. Whatever it was he never let on. It could have been a number of things and even some things he may not have known. Like our 55gal drums were taking on water, yes, they were leaking and I don't think any of us realized it. In other words the Unsinkable was sinking.

The motors were started and we were again under way. Hickman and other towns, then Memphis, Tennessee. What a magnificent city. My best memory of this place was the wall or dike that guarded the town from the river. It was 20-30 feet high and about two feet wide at the top. I had such great sea legs it was tough to walk on land, but I did walk the entire length of that wall. How crazy I was then. I would never allow my kids to climb that wall let alone walk on it.

Back on the raft and Greenville, Mississippi. Then the Arkansas River joined the Mississippi and we were 129 miles from Louisiana. We were behind schedule. A group meeting was called and we decided to make an all night run. Volunteers for the steering and lookout shifts were asked to sign up on the all night roster. The others were told to find a spot and dig in for the night. We did not have lights like the ones on your car only a small red (for the port side) light and a small green (starboard side) light. There was also a white light on top. These were not for us to see with but for others to see us.

To see the channel we used a large spotlight. When the spotlight hit a red buoy it would reflect and it looked like a cigar sticking out of the water. The black buoys would reflect flat on top. For me it was easier to see the buoys at night because I am very colorblind. We also used the blinking lights on the mile markers. If you let your eyes get accustomed to the dark you would be surprised how much you can see at night.

We picked a great night for this run and the river is completely different in the dark. As I took my turn as lookout I couldn't believe the beauty and might of the river. It was also a great time to just plain talk with each other about home, the river, school, our hopes, and fears, and our futures. It was great to just sit and watch the world from a position that not many people have had the opportunity to be in. I would love to do it again.

CHAPTER 12

For the Governor of Louisiana, Jimmy Davis, also of "You are My Sunshine" fame.

Remember how much each of us wanted to steer, or pilot in the beginning? By now the novelty had completely worn off. It was a constant battle to get some of the guys to take their watch. If they did not sell their watch they would just plain let go of the wheel and let us run aground or hit something. This was the most serious of infractions and these boys were dealt with harshly, not only by the staff, but the crew. Many fist fights broke out. Those who did volunteer to take the helm were rewarded by being excused from other duties. One such duty was fire wood collecting or washing dishes. This did not go over well with those who were sloughing off.

During the night two boys decided to head for home. They sneaked out of camp and started to hitchhike back to Minnesota. Jack was furious, we all watched him to see how he would handle this matter. There was an immediate group meeting and we were warned that this was unacceptable behavior. Not to mention how dangerous it could be this far from home and alone.

The boys were picked up the very next day and held in the Helena, Arkansas jail. Jack went there to straighten things out as we continued. You should have seen him when he returned the next day. He was all smiles and alone. We had another meeting and Jack announced that he made arrangements with the local sheriff to keep those clowns in jail until we finished the trip, no matter how long it took. That was just great. The punishment fit the crime and if there were any other ideas floating around about jumping ship they were put to rest then and there.

In 2001, 40 years after the trip, I spoke with these boys and to hear of their troubles after they left us was as hilarious as any comedy. Apparently the sheriff picked them up (Jack had tipped him off) and when he asked them who they were and where they were going, they tried to tell him in a phony southern accent that they were from a little plantation just down the road. I'll bet it was difficult for that man to keep a straight face. Not only was the accent terrible, but he knew that the boys were on the run. They spent the next twelve days in the Helena jail and were fed grits and gravy and given Bull Durham to smoke. They said raft food seemed mighty good after all. After their ordeal they were shipped home on a bus. Naturally, they jumped the bus in Chicago and hitchhiked home. By the way, they beat us back. You may as well know that the two boys were Mike A. and Mike B. they told me that they left, not so much because they hated the other boys or the trip, they just could not stand the confinement and close quarters, I guess I really cannot blame them for that. Mike A. passed away a few years ago and I was at his funeral in northeast Minneapolis. I met his parents, children and grandchildren. Mike talked about that raft trip almost every day of his life. I have read much of what Mark Twain wrote. I have also read much about Mr. Twain. I honestly believe that if the spirit of Huck Finn lived on into the 21st century, it lived on in Mike. I miss you Mike and I thank you for making me laugh at a time when I really needed it. I treasure the picture of you to this day, flinging your food overboard with a fork and a smirk and a smart ass comment, indeed one of my true heroes.

Somewhere during the next day most of us picked up a virus and it was impossible to move on. We pulled into Greenville, Mississippi and docked at the Greenville Yacht Club and were treated by a local doctor. We recovered and stayed long enough to pick up provisions and have our motors checked over. The newspaper people came down to the river and took our picture and we hit the front page of the Delta Democrat Times. That was July 16th 1961.

We set sail for Lake Providence and attended church. The Catholic boys went to Mass and the rest of us went to a Protestant church. In a small town we ran into a flagpole sitter. How odd I remember thinking, to spend your summer, or any time for that matter, sitting atop a flag pole in a box. He said he could see us coming down the river and he thought we were just as odd to do such a thing that we were doing. I hope he broke the record for his deed. I'll never know, in fact, don't even ask me if I care. I guess it takes all kinds.

Now for Vicksburg, Mississippi. The largest stern-wheeler ever made was docked there. The Sprague. It could push 64 loaded barges up the river. I was impressed. We were given a tour of this great boat and I could have stayed for another week and poked my nose into every corner of it. We had a tour of Vicksburg and ate a big meal in town. Then we were off to Baton Rouge.

Baton Rouge, Louisiana. The state capitol. A large crowd was on the banks to greet us and something was different. Something seemed wrong. Something was not right.

Someone yelled out from the crowd asking us if we were "Freedom Riders". When we told them we were on a pleasure cruise to New Orleans and had no idea what a "Freedom Rider" was, they took one look at our mode of transportation and did not believe one word. The next thing we knew we were being ushered into a paddy wagon, yes staff and all, and headed off to jail.

This was undoubtedly a first for the staff, but the rest of us took it in stride. We told them how to act during the booking process. Not even one grin. Fortunately, Jack was late getting to the marina with his car. When he found out what happened he was off to the poky like the Lone Ranger. Why heck, we never even got booked. Not only that the mayor came down and let us out of the holding cell and took us on a first class tour of the court house. We were also given the keys to the city and then driven to the state capitol building to meet the governor Mr. Jimmy Davis. Mr. Davis got his start in Minneapolis singing at the "Flame Room" he also wrote and recorded one of my favorite songs "You are My Sunshine". While we were in his office I jumped into his chair and declared myself to be the governor. Mr. Davis laughed and said that his Lt. Governor was out of town, so I could take his place. So there I was the Lt. Governor of the state of Louisiana for 45 minutes. What an honor to get to spend the day and have lunch with the Governor in the capitol building. Yes, we did get to present him with the Minnesota state flag and he in return gave us a state flag of Louisiana. This flag is still in the Fallon family and I hope that as it passes to the next generations this story will accompany it. Thank you Governor Jimmy Davis.

There will be no extra charge for this bit of information. In 1993 I went to Mogilev, Byelorussia to do some missionary work in the public schools. I taught the kids to sing, "You are My Sunshine" in English. That was a great thrill for me and I wish that Mr. Davis could have been there, he was still alive at that time.

Time to depart. A large amount of food was donated by the local merchants and as we loaded it onboard the news media was there taking pictures and interviewing us. Not far from our destination now, and the best is yet to come.

On the streets of
Hannibal, MO

Mike flinging food
and insults

Lift That Bale! Youngsters from Minnesota's Bar N o n e ranch, 13
miles north of A n o k a, carry watermel on,
peaches and bananas aboard their pontoon raft at Baton
Rouge, La. One group of boys made the Mississippi river
trip from Minneapolis to New Orleans, La., and will re-

turn by car. A second group of Bar-None youngsters is
now bringing the raft back to Minneapolis. Baton Rouge
merchants donated the food to the boys and Mayor Jack
Christian chatted with them about his Minnesota fishing
trips.

Loading supplies

Author far left

CHAPTER 13

For Colonel Richard Meinertzagen, C.B.E., D.S.O.

We backed into the current and passed under the Huey P. Long Bridge. We headed off to what became my favorite town on the river, White Castle, Louisiana. Yes, there really is a town called White Castle. We were treated like royalty there. We were taken on tours way back into bayou country and experienced the culture and the food, what great food. We had turtle soup, southern fried chicken, crayfish and much more. We visited John James Audubon's house and a plantation.

It was here that we played with Spanish moss. I have a neat picture of myself with a mass of moss covering my head. When I took it off and tossed it on the ground a very poisonous cottonmouth snake crawled out of the heap that was on my head just seconds before. How many times do you think I played with Spanish moss after that experience? Another claim to fame that White Castle boasted about was that they had the world's longest street.

It was in this town that a young man asked me if we were freedom riders. In the early 1960s people with too much time on their hands from the north would travel to the south and cause trouble. They usually rode the bus and that is how they got the name freedom riders. I didn't know what a freedom rider was then and I told that man so. He believed me and we became friends. He followed us around town and was very interested in our activities. Little did I know he was with the K.K.K. and was watching us to make sure that we didn't cause any trouble.

That was my first experience with a bigot and I didn't like it one bit. We had a group meeting later and discussed the way things were done here in the south back then. Jack had attended Tulane University in New Orleans, so he knew a few things. It bothered me. How could people who treated us so kindly treat black people so different? This has always bugged me and I have tried to judge people on their actions rather than on the color of their skin. No matter, as I said, White Castle was still my favorite place and we, at least I, wasn't finished with it yet.

We left town and went a little ways down stream and set up camp. Just after bedtime I felt a pain in my gut. I thought that the virus had finally caught up with me, but the pain was so great that the staff figured they better get me to a doctor. Two staff and one crew member, for a lookout, took me back to White Castle on the raft. I was taken to the local hospital in the city ambulance. I remember looking out the window and seeing the lettering on the side window advertising that it was not only the city ambulance, but the hearse and laundry truck to boot.

When we arrived at the hospital I was still in my sleeping bag. When the doctor asked me to get out of it I refused. When I was asked why not by my staff member I had to tell him that I didn't have any clothes on. They had to run back and get my pants. How embarrassing. Hey, it was hot out at night in the south what else did they expect? It was decided that I had had an appendix attack. The doctor said I should stay overnight. Merle stayed with me in a small hotel and we relaxed for the next day and one more night.

The doctors' name was Dr. Percy LaBlanc and several years later, after the raft trip, I saw his wife on a TV game show called "I've Got a Secret". I don't remember what her secret was, but it was fun to see some one I knew on TV.

Merle and I took the bus to Donaldsonville, Louisiana and rejoined the crew. It was now that Merle left us and headed for a wedding, his own. He and Mavis will celebrate their 50th anniversary this year. Happy anniversary you two, and many more. Three cheers for them.

That night we camped near Donaldsonville. While in Donaldsonville Jack ask Jerry and me if we would help carry some supplies back to the raft from a local store. It was hot that day and as we sat on the back shipping dock. Jack bought the three of us a bottle of pop. A Black man who helped carry out the boxes was standing there so Jack bought him a pop also. A white fellow came around the corner and saw the four of us enjoying our soda. He ask the black man how he got the soda and the man nodded at Jack. That "man" looked at Jack and said, "Don't you never buy a N... nothing". Jack told Jerry and me to take our boxes to the raft and he would be along shortly. About ten minutes later Jack was walking toward the raft with his box of supplies and, holy mackerel, did he have a shiner. He just said to Jerry and I not to worry and not to mention anything. I sure would hate to have seen the other guy. The only problem I had was wondering if life got any worse for that poor black fellow.

Not far downstream from our campsite was a ferry crossing. The ferryboat ran 24 hours a day and my buddy, Eddie and I decided to check it out. We went through the woods and went aboard the boat. It was not very big; it only had room for about eight cars. We introduced ourselves to the captain and he said he had heard of us and was honored to have us aboard. The ride was free and as we rode across the river, Eddie and I hatched a plan to get out of pitching our mosquito netting for the night. We talked to the captain and filled him in on our idea and he gave us the go ahead. Eddie and I went back to the raft and got our sleeping bags and rode that ferryboat back and forth across the river all night long. Not many people can say they have ever done that. What fun! Next stop, New Orleans.

CHAPTER 14

For Mr. Karl Hoerschgen, my 11th & 12th grade English teacher.

Daybreak and we were up and excited. We got out our cleanest clothes and packed everything away as neat as we could. Out into the channel and in a few miles New Orleans. There were indeed times that I thought we would never make it this far. The weather, the current, the hidden things in the water, and the raft itself, at times seemed to be against us. In spite of the pitch, yaw, and roll of our craft not one of us got seasick. But we hung in there and we had succeeded.

I had learned much from this experience, as I have mentioned before. Certainly we all had learned a lot, both us boys and the staff had great on the job training. As much as I had learned from the river, I believe I learned more from the staff, Dennis, Merle, Ron and Jack. Most of all I learned how to make do with what was at hand and that griping and complaining about your circumstances never makes them better.

One important thing I learned was to take responsibility for my actions. In the harbors and marinas where we tied up at times, there were signs saying, "Slow No Wake". That meant you could not make waves behind your boat. If anyone got hurt or anything got broken because of your wake it was **your fault** and you had to make things right. Our raft did not go fast enough for us to worry about our wake, but we were aware of it at all times. It's the same way with your life. You must be aware of your wake, or actions, or the things that you do that affect others, you are responsible for them and if you harm or offend someone you must accept your responsibility and make things right.

Many times on this trip we tried to blame one another for things that went wrong when it was our own fault. Some of us grew up and sadly, some did not. We had all taken turns as lookouts, (both fore and aft), pilots, navigators, cooks, mechanics, housekeepers, inventors, explorers, survivors, and in a sense modern day pioneers. I would put these boys up against any sailor, perhaps not in the strength department, but as far as knowledge and first hand experience. We passed the test, we were able-bodied seamen. We conquered the Mighty Mississippi.

Several boats started to gather around us as we neared the city. They were full of well-wishers and news media. One boat had a crew from Sports Illustrated Magazine and they took pictures of us and we hit the cover of the next issue. They sailed along side us and interviewed us for quite a while, but we really wanted to get to our destination. The river was bigger than life. Here we were on this tiny homemade raft competing with barges, pleasure craft, ferryboats, and now huge sea going vessels. The raft was noticeably bowed and we knew some of the oil drums were water logged. It was time to get off of the river and we knew it.

There it was, New Orleans. The Crescent City. Three cheers for us. Three cheers for the staff. Three cheers for New Orleans. And three cheers for the river. It was about four miles from our sight of the city, that we stopped. It was at the foot of Canal Street at the ferry docks. There were lots of people there, but not all of them were there to greet us. They were waiting for the ferry and we were in the way. We could not stay there or the ferry or the waves from other river traffic would crush us. We would have to go down river about eight miles to the intracostal waterway then enter the inner harbor navigation canal that led to Lake Pontchartrain.

Now it was dark and we had to go through another lock. This lock was not on the river, but between the river and Lake Pontchartrain. Jack had gone ahead to make arrangements. The Lockmaster asked us if we had ever been through a lock before and we all laughed. He thought that we were a group of Sea Scouts from above New Orleans and when he learned that we had come from Minnesota he asked permission to come aboard. We said yes and he climbed down the ladder and shook hands with each one of us. This canal went right through the industrial area of New Orleans and we had to be very careful. These people were working and we were in the way. Five miles later we were on the lake.

We passed the airport and an amusement park on our final four or five miles to the Southern Yacht Club. It was beautiful to see the lights of that park and the city in the background. We also saw flying fish, it was fun to watch them try to fly or jump across our bow. Jack met us at the yacht club and we tied up and made camp in the West End Park across the street from Lake Pontchartrain.

CHAPTER 15

For Henry and Mildred Stivland

Yes, here we were in New Orleans. Or should I say that we were in culture shock? I'm not going to spend a lot of time telling you about New Orleans. It is a beautiful city and we covered most of it. I would like to share with you some of the highlights, events and lessons I learned thus far. Also, remember the other crew was on the way down from Minneapolis to take our places and take the raft up the river home.

First, the raft was in terrible shape. At least five of the barrels were full of water and needed to be replaced. The brackets that held them in place did not function as they were designed and you had to undo almost each one just to get at the one that needed to be changed. These barrels or drums varied in length by at least three inches, so it was difficult to make a perfect fit. They were also out of alignment and don't forget, the whole thing was bent and they were binding in the center. Jack found some people with the know how to get the thing fixed and while we toured New Orleans the Unsinkable was being repaired. We were also sailing on salt water now and I think that didn't do the motors any good. More about them later.

We were camped within sight of the world's longest bridge (26 miles to be exact). We were taken to Bay Saint Louis, Mississippi in a car caravan and we rode over the bridge. We were allowed to play and swim in the Gulf of Mexico. Some of us thought that New Orleans was right on the Gulf, but it is about 100 miles away and that is why we rode in cars. We met with the mayor and received the keys to the city. We were given about .75 cents every day for food and that was plenty. I usually got a poor boy sandwich for .35 cents and that would make two meals. A poor boy is like a sub or hero sandwich that we eat here.

One day we were checking out the ferryboats at the foot of Canal Street where we first landed. It was great fun to watch the pickpockets working the crowds. They weren't very good at it and most of us could spot them right away as they bumped into people. The police knew who most of them were and they would take them off to jail and they would be back the same day, over and over. We did get into some mischief and I got my first, and last, chew of tobacco. To this day if I see someone chewing that junk I start to gag.

We made friends with a fellow who lived on a boat at the yacht club and his boat had sunk in Lake Pontchartrain just before we arrived. Some of us went out to help him recover his belongings by scuba diving. One item he brought to the surface was his electric coffeepot. I'll never forget him looking at the bottom of the pot and reading, "Do not submerge in water". He just laughed and plugged it in and it still worked. I wish I knew the brand name on the thing, it sure would make a great sales pitch.

One day while I was passing the time by fishing in the "toilet" in the marina at the yacht club I saw a hammerhead shark swim under the raft. I wonder what I would have done if I would have caught him.

While in town I noticed that some of the public drinking fountains were absolutely filthy. I remember wondering why no one cleaned them, perhaps they were broken, I thought. Then I noticed a black gentleman getting a drink from one of these fountains and being as I was thirsty, I waited for him to finish and then I stepped up and started to get a drink. How was I to know this was a big no, no. A white man grabbed me by the neck and asked me if I knew how to read and when I said "Yes" he pointed out the sign over the fountain, it read "Colored". I told the man that I didn't know what that meant and he wised me up real fast. Black people had their own places in the South and I had better get smart or else I would be in a lot of trouble.

This was a sad day for me. Several of my friends back home were Black and many were American Indians. They were never treated any different than any other of my friends. Three of the kids on our crew were Indian and the only thing different about them to me was their beautiful last names. The more I saw of this attitude toward black people the more I hated it. I was only a kid and there was nothing that I could do. I felt very ashamed of being white and I wanted to apologize to every black person that I met. I still feel the same way today all these years later. Things have changed in the south, but they could always be better. The only thing that I can do is live my life and treat others the way I would like to be treated.

The new crew arrived and we had one big group meeting. The crew taking the raft home would be fewer in order to lighten the load. Of the original crew there were 13 of us left and there were only seven replacements. It was decided that four crew members from the original crew would chosen to help get the Unsinkable home. The staff called for volunteers and believe it or not four of us raised our hands. Yes, I was one of those crazy volunteers. Now, I would be going up the river for real.

CHAPTER 16

For the boys and girls of Mogilev.

The original crew was now headed for home. I got to tour New Orleans all over again with the new crew. All together I spent twelve days in that great city. The raft was again seaworthy and we were off. Across Lake Pontchartrain and through the canal and one lock and onto the Mississippi. What fun to watch these new "Green" guys as they took the wheel and learned the ropes and the way of the river.

Our goal was to be home in the same amount of time it took to get down the river. Well, ha, ha, ha. Remember, we only made 12 MPH on the way down and now we were fighting the current with a bent raft. We were making only ten miles per day. At that rate I think we would still be out there today trying to get home. I enjoyed sharing my knowledge of the river with the new crew. At times they would listen and then at other times they would not. Like me they had to learn the hard way. These boys were older than the first crew and sometimes they did not like to be told what to do or how to do it by younger kids like me. I have seen this attitude ever since then in people who just start a new job or are just learning to drive. I call people like this "know it all's". You will run into these people everywhere you go in your life and even though I don't pretend to know everything, however, when I offer advise to these morons and I get any static from them, I shut down immediately and put as much distance between myself and them. A great name for them is implacable, that means they will never learn.

For many years I was a trainer for a large warehouse company and I would like you to know that even though I was as nice as I could be to these trainees, most of them were never invited back to work the next season. We must be able to take advice from people who have been trained in certain areas and we must listen to our parents and loved ones. Believe me they want to help you to be a success as much as you want to be one.

The staff onboard that summer also taught me to be patient with the new guys as they were patient with me, I hope to pass this along even today. During our battle to go upstream we burned out two more motors. The Scott Outboard Company was right there to give us new motors. That made a total of five engines. A cost I would estimate at close to well over $50,000 in today's money.

It took us ten days to reach Baton Rough, only 100 miles up river from New Orleans. We knew we would never make it home via the river. A meeting was called and Jack broke the news. The new guys weren't as attached to the raft and they had had their fun and were ready to go home. I was disappointed, but I knew that it would be impossible to travel any more on the Unsinkable. We stayed in Baton Rouge and packed our gear and arrangements were made for us to take the bus home. I don't remember the trip home. I must have slept. It was nice not to keep a lookout and let some one else do the driving.

I do remember stopping in Chicago, Illinois and the staff warning us not to take off. No one did. You may have noticed that each chapter has been dedicated to someone. These are or have been real people. Some famous and others not so. Each one of these people has been a hero to me at one time or another. I believe we should all have heroes. Not to worship, but to look up to and for inspiration. There have been many, many heroes, but only one true celebrity, the Lord Jesus Christ. Should I live to be one thousand years old I will never buy the asinine idea that you are a product of your environment. Your environment is a product of you and only you.

I know a man who drove a Hostess Cup Cake truck for 40 years. This man does not even know that he is a hero to me. He is one of my heroes because in all the years that he drove that truck he never complained about his job. He has a nice wife and three kids my age. When he was younger he and his wife took in foster kids until they could be placed in a permanent home. Perhaps you have a hero or better yet you may even be a hero. A hero does not have to be strong or rich, or black, or white, they just have to be someone you admire for any reason. They can be a relative or a stranger, it's up to you. See what you can come up with and maybe you can start a hobby of collecting heroes. I'll even bet you could be a hero if you don't think you are one, then start to think of ways that you could be one. You don't need to sail down a river like I did to be a hero and that trip did not make me a hero, but I do hope that I am a hero at least to my own children and granddaughter, Kate.

The raft was hoisted onto a barge and brought back to Minneapolis. There it was dismantled and the barrels were sold for $2.00 each. The motors were returned and the logs that we kept were also turned over to the Scott Company. We salvaged what we could and scrapped the rest, the Unsinkable was no more.

EPILOGUE

I t was the beginning of the school year, 1961. I had just turned 15. Tenth grade. "What did you do on your summer vacation Dean?"........"Ya, Right!". It was also back to the weekend program. There we sat in a small room, about 15 of us kids and two or three staff members, it was announced to us that we needed to come up with a plan for next summers vacation. We were told that if we did not come up with a plan we would spend the summer as guests at the Hennepin County Home School in Glen Lake, Minnesota. Yes, there was another raft trip in 1962.

Instead of going to New Orleans the trip was from Minneapolis to St. Louis and return. We traveled on a manufactured pontoon boat donated by Kayot. It was also factory modified to our specs, an extra shorter pontoon was factory installed between the starboard and port pontoons. We had a real seat to sit on to steer from. Scott donated two more outboards. They were smaller, only 28 horsepower each, with a different power pitch. They worked fine. This pontoon was used again in 1963 while I attended summer school.

In 1964 the Weeres Company of St. Cloud, Minnesota donated an enormous five-pontoon platform. We built the superstructure from donated materials and would you believe an aluminum roof? Two more motors were given to us, again by Scott, they were very small, only 14 horses each. They were called Ox motors and were experimental and they not only had a power pitch they had 12 inch blades on the props. These worked just great.

I had graduated from high school in June and was no longer in the weekend program. All of the staff was new and so was the crew. I was asked by Hennepin County if I would like to go along and be the cook. They offered to paid me a stipend of two dollars per week and I jumped at the chance. This was quite an honor for me. I hope that the county never finds out that I would have paid them the two bucks and still have done the cooking.

Each of these trips was as much fun and exciting as the first. Altogether I logged just over 5,000 miles on the Mississippi and passed through each lock at least five times. I've made life long friends and memories. The river changes every day, just like you and me. It never, ever, gets boring.

Just after the last trip in 1964 I joined the US Navy. Compared to the raft trips the Navy was a piece of cake. I have waited 50 years to tell this story in print and indeed it has been a labor of love. Most stories wind up with, "The End", but not this one.

Thank you.

For more info visit us online at:
http://www.NewOrleansOrSunk.com

The unsinkables

In the manner of modern-day Huck Finns, 13 boys (ranging in age from 11 to 14) traveled down the Mississippi by raft this summer—from Minneapolis to New Orleans. Sponsored by The Volunteers of America, the youngsters assembled a 33-by-16-foot platform, floated it on 40 oil drums, added a canvas shelter and dubbed the craft *The Unsinkable*. Before the boys and their counselors cast off, two outboard motors were hooked onto the raft's stern, and —although Huck doubtless would have sneered—all hands donned life jackets.

Along the way, the youngsters stopped at Hannibal, Mo. (Mark Twain's boyhood home) and visited such historic river towns as Memphis, Vicksburg and Natchez. They met no desperadoes, but they did share an adventure: one 13-year-old successfully underwent an emergency appendectomy. After a month and some 1,700 miles of water, the boys arrived in New Orleans. Piped up Eddie Caton, 13, a youngster Huck would have cottoned to: "I'd do it again in a minute."

SPORTS ILLUSTRATED   SEPTEMBER 4, 1961

I Like Matthew 10:8b

Dean Felsing is in the Minneapolis Buildings and Grounds Department.

"Freely ye have received, freely give."

Having been in trouble with the law, I was living at Bar-None Boys' Ranch in the winter of 1961. Fifteen boys and I built a raft and floated down the Mississippi River to New Orleans that summer. In 1962 and 1964 I made similar trips to St. Louis and returned via the river. I found that after these trips I couldn't share my experiences with other people. They wouldn't accept the wild (but true) stories of my river adventures.

In 1963 I went to Youth For Christ Lifeline Camp and found out what it meant to be a Christian, but I wouldn't accept Christ for myself. It was just too fantastic that Christ would do the things for me that people said he could. During the 1964 raft trip, I realized I could never really share my experiences without him. When we returned, I accepted Christ and he changed the direction of my life from downstream to upstream.

Since then it has been my dream to share my experiences with other fellows who are heading in the same direction I was. I believe these trips can be used to reach boys for Christ rather than just to give them pleasure. Christ has made my dream a reality; now I have a 21-foot pontoon boat, and plan to use it for boys who need Christ. As Christ freely gave to me, I want to freely give him to boys who are in need. ☐

Courtesy BGEA